Heart and Soul Pieces
A Mystical Journey of Healing and Self Recovery

DELFINA ALDEN

HEART AND SOUL PIECES

A MYSTICAL journey of HEALING and SELF recovery

DELFINA ALDEN

Cover and book design by Delfina Alden

Original artwork and poetry by Delfina Alden

Published in association with World Changing Warriors Media Group
www.worldchangingwarriors.com

For questions and bulk sales, contact author.

www.heartandsoulpiecesbook.com

www.delfinaalden.com

ISBN: 978-1532860423

10 9 8 7 6 5 4 3 2 1

This book is dedicated to My parents, Alex and Oksana.

You two started me off on a journey of rebelliousness, revelry in the experience of the unknown and constant self discovery at a very young age.

To you, my dear ones, I am always grateful.

And now, it has come circle, as you had written a poem to commemorate my birth, papa, and you reread it to me many times, mama, I dedicate this book and my poetry to commemorate our journey together, thus far.

BEFORE YOU BEGIN: go to heartandsoulpiecesbook.com/freegift and download the "Heart and Soul Healing Package." This is a set of metaphysically empowered guided meditations and healing sessions that I have packaged specifically for you to use along with this book. Using these will help you tune in even deeper and get way more powerful results!

Go, right now, it's super important that you get this asap because it's only available free for a limited time during the launch of this book.

This is my free gift to you. I usually sell these in my Warrior Shop but because I love gifts and because I know that this powerful, energy infused guided meditation and healing session set will help you tremendously in the work you're embarking on in this book, I'm giving them away as a little "I love you" prezzie. And, since we're getting to know each other better; I think it's mega important to establish that I LOVE prezzies very much, especially giving them!

Go to heartandsoulpiecesbook.com/freegift and download your free audio mp3 meditation gifts right now. You'll be using them a lot throughout this book.

www.heartandsoulpieces.com

Preface (read this, it's important!)

This book was created for you, but it is also being created by you. This book is a living record of your precious journey in this particular moment in time. It is no accident that you hold this text in your hand. Something, many things, everything about what you're experiencing right now, have experienced up until this point, begs to be documented. More than that, you are at a crossroads. You hear a calling from deep within and you want to strengthen it. You want to understand it. You want to merge with it. You know it holds a key to your wholeness, to your deepest inner knowing.

This book was carefully crafted to help you achieve that elusive goal. It was created both in an instant and over many years. The poetry and drawings are ones I've been creating and carefully keeping safe for years, waiting for the moment when I could finally share them with you. They chronicle a part of my journey, the most sacred part of my journey, the time when I was broken open for the first time. The time I call "the end of lies and the beginning of the many truths." To say it was a special time would be a grave understatement. It was magical, it was magnificent. It was transcendent.

I share these creations, these pieces of my heart and soul in order to help you share your deepest secrets. I am taking the first step. I am opening myself to you. I am showing you my darkest inner dwellings. I am revealing words, emotions, sentiments and secrets no one has ever seen. By revealing me, by revealing this part of my journey, I hope to empower you to reveal your innermost truths. Perhaps to yourself at first, and then, if and when you're ready, to others and the world at large.
Please, take your time, awakening, blooming and blossoming is a process.

When you complete this book, you will have a written record of your journey. You will have a manual to the deeper inner workings of your psyche and your soul. You will have a collection of love notes from you, to you. You will have many answers. You will have a living record documenting your legendary existence. Again, just to remind you, this book was created for you but it is also being created by you, right now.

This book and everything in it is my gift to you. This is a gift offered from the very depths of me, a collection of the pieces of my heart and soul, with love and reverence for the infinite divine power in you.

This is your book and this is your journey. The fact that you're holding it in your hands means that you're ready to delve deeper into it.

I invite you to begin to do so now.

Ready?

And so, we begin.

I'm going to ask you to make a sacred commitment to yourself. And, I'm going to ask that you to keep it. I am going to ask you to remember, for the duration of this journey, and hopefully forever after, that you are your greatest treasure and that the most important commitment you can make is to yourself.

You are the chosen one, you are the one you have been waiting for, you are the savior and your most beloved.

With that in mind, I offer up a sacred contract. You'll see it on the next page and you can either keep it in this book or tear it out and hang it somewhere you can see it daily in order to remind you about your commitment to treat every part of your Self with sacred kindness and love.

I,   am embarking on a
sacred journey, guided by my heart and soul and led gently by
a soul sister.

I promise to be loving, supportive, and generous with myself on
this path. I vow to accept and acknowledge all that comes
forward and to embrace it with loving kindness. I accept the
truth, the knowing and the unexpected abundance that is bound
to flow into my life starting from this moment forward.

I now allow it to spill out into my daily life and spill over
into the world, blessing and uplifting every being that I
encounter.

With Love Eternal,

Dated

How to Use This Book

You are free to use it any way you want to, of course, but I do have a few suggestions. My first suggestion is that you keep the things you write in to this book safe and hidden. You may choose to share this later on, but for now, while we are in the process of unfolding, keep it sacred, keep it safe. The format and the layout have been organized in a way which allows me to first open up to you and reveal my heart and soul via my creative outpouring (the poetry and drawings) before asking you to open up your heart and soul. This is a journey book, meaning this book literally takes you on a journey into not only my heart and soul, your heart and soul but also the collective Heart and Soul at large to which we are all intrinsically linked. If you're open to it, I invite you to follow the journey from start to finish as it is laid out. If you do this, a mystical, magical miracle will occur. This, I promise, this I vow, healing will occur, if only you allow.

The Drawings

Each drawing can be described as a deconstructed mandala which was created by me in a meditative trance state. They are imbued with very specific energy and observing them will bring about positive, transformative results. Use these mystical drawings as a visual meditation tool by staring into the depths of each one individually. As you do so, you may find yourself being transported into another realm, one of limitless possibility and uninterrupted flow. After viewing the deconstructed mandala, record your observations on the provided pages marked "Thoughts * Impressions * Musings * Flow." This artwork serves as a doorway into a deeper level of Us. As a side note, I have these drawings, the originals, hanging in my bedroom and I do this same exercise I describe here, quite often.

The Poetry

The mystical verses are the next step in the opening and unfolding of the doors within. As you may already know, there are codes within codes in each phrase and every word and when the encoded words are weaved together, magic occurs. Breathe in a deep inhale, read the poem and exhale all that begs to be released. Use this as a clearing exercise. The poems are arranged in a way that takes you on a journey, one with a beginning and an end. The end, in turn serves as a beginning.

The poem journey sets you up for your personal journey throughout the book. There are pages provided after each poem for you to record your thoughts, observations and any flow that comes forward. Use them and I promise you will surprise and delight yourself with what emerges.

Your Journey

The third part of the book is your personal journey. It is formatted to serve as a workbook, playbook, mystical-transformational instrument of healing, recovery and creation. There are questions I will ask that are crucial for you to answer honestly, writing prompts that are critical to embark upon, and rituals that I recommend you perform, but those are optional. This book is meant to be used. It is meant to be used up completely. I recommend you use it daily until you run out of ways to use it. These are so much more than simply words on paper, they are indeed your hero's/heroine's journey, chronicled and empowered by mysticism that dances like holy fire in order to empower your purpose and potential. Allow it to do just that.

Thoughts * Impressions * Musings * Flow

Thoughts * Impressions * Musings * Flow

Thoughts * Impressions * Musings * Flow

Thoughts * Impressions * Musings * Flow

Thoughts * Impressions * Musings * Flow

Thoughts * Impressions * Musings * Flow

Thoughts * Impressions * Musings * Flow

Thoughts * Impressions * Musings * Flow

Thoughts * Impressions * Musings * Flow

SOMEONE CAME AND OPENED UP A HEAVY DOOR
AND AS IT SLOWLY TURNED
THE KNOB, IT BROKE
AND SO THE DOOR MUST NOW REMAIN COMPLETELY
OPEN
AS TO ALLOW THE LIGHT TO ENTER IN
THE SUN TO GLEAM
AND AIR AND OXYGEN TO CIRCULATE
AT ONCE REMOVING OLD STALE ODORS
AND BRINGING IN SUCH NEW AND UNFAMILIAR SCENTS
BECAUSE THIS DOOR WAS LOCKED FOR MANY EONS
THE DUST COLLECTED THERE HAS MUCH TO TELL
AND SO AS IF BY MAGIC THE REMOVAL OF AN EVIL SPELL
ALL OF THE YEARS OF SOLITUDE AND LONGING ARE NOW
RELEASED AND FINALLY THE ROOM CAN BREATHE
A LONG AND LOVINGLY EXHALED SIGH OF RELIEF
THE SENTENCE THAT ONCE SEEMED ETERNAL
HAS BEEN REMOVED AND NOW THE SPACE
IS FREE AND READY TO BE FILLED

-DELFINA 2/2012

Thoughts * Impressions * Musings * Flow

Thoughts * Impressions * Musings * Flow

Thoughts * Impressions * Musings * Flow

LOOK INTO THE MIRROR
STARE INTO YOUR REFLECTION
WHO'S FACES THAT?
FURROWED BROW
FEATURES UNRECOGNIZABLE
SKIN FULL OF ENLARGED PORES
WIDE, DEEP, HUNGRY
OPEN AS IF DESPERATELY TRYING TO DRINK
IT ALL IN BEFORE IT'S TOO LATE
THOSE EYES
DO THEY STILL SPARKLE?
HAVE THEY EVER?
OR WAS THAT YET ANOTHER LIE THAT YOU BELIEVED
ABOUT YOURSELF
ISN'T IT SO HUMBLING TO BE TRUTHFUL
BRUTALLY HONEST WITH WHAT YOU REALLY SEE
IN THE MIRROR, WHEN YOU TAKE TIME TO REALLY
REFLECT
SOME MAY SAY NO, IT IS IN FACT, TERRIFYING
OTHERS MAY ARGUE FOR HOW LIBERATING IT IS
WHAT DO YOU SAY?
WHAT DO YOU SEE?
LOOK!

-DELFINA 10/2011

Thoughts * Impressions * Musings * Flow

Thoughts * Impressions * Musings * Flow

Thoughts * Impressions * Musings * Flow

THE WITHDRAW FELT BY ME
FROM LOSING YOU IS SO AKIN
TO THAT OF ANY POTENT DRUG
WHICH FILLS THE VEINS AND SPREADS
SO QUICKLY THROUGH THE CELLS
AND SETTLES IN THE MUSCLES
MAKING THEM CONTRACT AND FLEX
I KNOW TOO WELL
OF WHAT COMES NEXT
THE SADNESS, SHAME AND LONGING
FOR MY WILLPOWER
OH BUT THE WILLINGNESS
AND THE DESIRE
JUST TO FEEL IT ONE MORE TIME
TO FEEL THE THRILL OF THE EXPERIENCE
THE HIGH, AND THE EXCITEMENT OF
INGESTING YOU ONCE MORE
AND LETTING THE SENSATIONS OF
YOUR TOUCH UPON MY SKIN
ALLOWING THE FULL WEIGHT
OF YOUR STRONG HANDS
ENVELOPING MY WRISTS
AND PULLING ME TO YOU
EMBRACING MY ENTIRE BEING
AND HOLDING ME FOR EVEN A SPLIT SECOND
AND HEAVEN KNOWS WHAT I WOULD
GIVE AWAY OR TRADE OR SELL
JUST FOR THAT MOMENT OF PURE PLEASURE
OF FEELING YOUR EMBRACE
THE LOOK THAT SPREADS ACROSS YOUR FACE
AS YOU TAKE IN THE SWEET AROMA

OF OUR ENERGIES COLLIDING, INTERTWINING
AND THEN EXPLODING IN A MOMENT OF
PURE BLISS
WHAT I WOULDN'T DO IN THIS
ONE OF MY DESPERATE MOMENTS
TO DRINK YOU IN AND FEEL MY BODY
GO INSANE, OR SIMPLY HEAR YOU
WHISPERING MY NAME
AND YET, I'M SAVORING THIS PAIN
IT'S SO FAMILIAR, YES I KNOW IT WELL
I CLOSE MY EYES AND I SIT STILL
EXPERIENCING EACH AND EVERY TINY
BURST OF THE DISCOMFORT OF THIS
AT ONCE SEEMINGLY MY TYPICAL WITHDRAWAL
BUT HERE'S THE DIFFERENCE, THIS IS WHY
I FEAR I MAY NOT MAKE IT OUT THIS TIME
WHEN IT GETS REALLY BAD AND I AM ON THE FLOOR
CONVULSING, BEGGING FOR A HIT
THERE IS NO DEALER IN THE WORLD
NO MATTER HOW THEY TRIED
THAT CAN SELL ME EVEN HALF A GRAM OF YOU

-DELFINA 12/2011

Thoughts * Impressions * Musings * Flow

Thoughts * Impressions * Musings * Flow

I AM A DELICATE FLOWER
AND YET I FLOW WITH INFINITE POWER
FROM THE STEM TO THE LEAF
TO THE UNFOLDING BUDS (WHICH OPENS GENTLY WITH
GREAT PURPOSE)
I AM UNSTOPPABLE

-DELFINA 2013

Thoughts * Impressions * Musings * Flow

Thoughts * Impressions * Musings * Flow

Thoughts * Impressions * Musings * Flow

I READ MY HOROSCOPE TODAY
IT TOLD ME
YOU WERE IN MY FUTURE
IT SPOKE OF LOVELY DAYS TO COME
I LISTENED
AND IT MADE ME CALM
I DO NOT KNOW
IF SEERS, MAGICIANS AND TRUTH SAYERS
CAN PREDICT
ALL THAT I SEE AHEAD OF ME
I SEE IT CLEARLY
ALL OF THE FOG THAT PERMEATED
HERE FOR OH SO LONG
THAT FOG IS GONE

-DELFINA 2012

Thoughts * Impressions * Musings * Flow

Thoughts * Impressions * Musings * Flow

Thoughts * Impressions * Musings * Flow

NOW MY SPIRIT IS FREE
IN THIS MOMENT OF ME
TRUTH AND LIGHT'S ALL I SEE
IT ENCOMPASSES ME
IT ALLOWS ME TO BE
IT'S JUST ME AND THE SEA
AND THE AIR THAT I BREATHE
I CAN FEEL PRECIOUS LIQUID
AS IT FILLS TO THE BRIM
OH THIS SCENT SO DIVINE
IT HAS DETOXED MY MIND
IT ALLOWS ME TO BE
OPENS WIDE EYES FOR ME
IT ALLOWS ALL THE GOOD THINGS
TO RISE FROM WITHIN
FOSTERS FREEDOM FROM WORRY
REMOVES EVERY FEAR AS IT BATHES ME IN TRUTH
I FEEL JOY, I AM FREE

-DELFINA 2013

Thoughts * Impressions * Musings * Flow

Thoughts * Impressions * Musings * Flow

Thoughts * Impressions * Musings * Flow

Your Journey So Far: Healing, Revealing, Restoring and Discovering.

What are 3 things you are happy with and are grateful for right now, in this moment?

And now, list 3 more...

And 2 more...

Thoughts * Impressions * Musings * Flow

What are 3 milestones that you've reached so far this year?

#3

#2

#1

Thoughts * Impressions * Musings * Flow

What are the major milestones of your life, so far?

What makes these milestones significant? Why do they matter to you?

What makes you significant?

Thoughts * Impressions * Musings * Flow

Have you celebrated these achievements?

In what ways? How do you celebrate?

If you haven't really celebrated, why not?

Choose one achievement you're absolutely giddy about. Now, tell me how you're going to celebrate.

Do it. Right now. Go.

How do YOU deserve to be celebrated?

How do you DESIRE to be celebrated?

We shall create a celebration, right now, in this moment, describe what it looks like, feels like, smells like.

Who is in attendance?

What are you wearing?

Pick a date for your Grand Celebration.
Write the date below.

Commit to it.
Create it.

Thoughts * Impressions * Musings * Flow

Thoughts * Impressions * Musings * Flow

What do you want to be sure to remember?

Oh, YES. Please tell me more, spill the deets...

What would you really rather forget?

Why?

Thoughts * Impressions * Musings * Flow

Thoughts * Impressions * Musings * Flow

How do you want to FEEL on a daily basis?

Yes, and.....

YES to all of this. Go further, describe your perfect day...

What gives you this feeling you've so eloquently described?

Draw this feeling, preferably in full color.

What makes you feel Joyous and completely Alive?

How does this activity or experience feed your heart and soul?

Thoughts * Impressions * Musings * Flow

If you were to choose only one way to feel for the rest of this year, what would that one feeling be?

What does a day feeling this one emotion look like? Describe it in detail on the following page.

Thoughts * Impressions * Musings * Flow

This year, you will feel:

You will come to embody this feeling.

Write it out again.
Commit to this.
Say it out loud right now.
Live it.

And now, that this is your True North, the whispers of your soul sent via encoded love notes.

Thoughts * Impressions * Musings * Flow

What would you like to have way more of in your life?

Why?

How does this question and your answer to it make your body feel?

Close your eyes, breathe in and ask again.

What would you like to create in service to the world?

More details please? What does this look like?

Thoughts * Impressions * Musings * Flow

Why is it absolutely crucial that you do this, that you create this change in service to the world? Why is this work important?

How would it make you feel to live in that reality, the one you describe, on a daily basis?

What must change (within and outside of you) right now in order for you to welcome this reality into being?

Are you ready to allow these changes to occur?

What is destined to become your legacy?

What were you created to create?

Why are YOU the ONE that MUST do this?
(you feel it in your bones and you know it to be true!)

Thoughts * Impressions * Musings * Flow

Go back through the pages and read what you've written so far.

Do you notice a pattern?

Do you recognize your beauty and your brilliance?

Are you ready to go deeper?

Thoughts * Impressions * Musings * Flow

AND NOW A RITUAL, AN INITIATION...

THE DOOR IS NOW WIDE OPEN AND YOU ARE BEING USHERED IN TO YOUR IDEAL PRESENT. CLOSE YOUR EYES, INHALE DEEPLY, EXHALE SLOWLY AND REPEAT "I ALLOW" THREE TIMES.

USE THE "ACCESS YOUR DIVINE SELF TUNE-IN TO YOUR HEART AND SOUL" GUIDED MEDITATION TO TUNE IN DEEPER.
(THE ONE I GAVE YOU AS A FREE GIFT, VISIT WWW.HEARTANDSOULPIECESBOOK.COM FOR INFO)

NOW, IMAGINE THE POSSIBILITIES. WHAT IS ON THE OTHER SIDE OF THE DOOR? WHAT DOES IT LOOK LIKE, SMELL LIKE, FEEL LIKE, SOUND LIKE?

ON THE FOLLOWING PAGE, DESCRIBE IN DETAIL WHAT YOU SEE, SENSE AND EXPERIENCE ON THE OTHER SIDE OF THE DOOR, THE SIDE THAT IS YOUR IDEAL PRESENT. YOU MAY USE WORDS OR DRAW PICTURES OF WHAT YOU SEE.

TAKE THIS TIME TO LAY OUT THE FOUNDATION FOR CREATING ALL YOUR BEAUTIFUL HEART DESIRES.

Draw, write out and bring in to the physical that which you sensed and saw while performing the initiation ritual on the previous page.

Thoughts * Impressions * Musings * Flow

Self Love Infused Preparation for Brilliance Ritual:

Pour yourself a bath. If you don't have access to a bathtub, create a foot soak using this recipe.

Toss in:

Two handfuls of sea salt

One handful of baking soda

10 drops of lavender oil

10 drops of rosemary oil

Close your eyes and soak in the concoction for at least 15-20 minutes. Allow the brilliance to soak in and all doubts to wash away. Languish in the space of self love, renewed hope, and rejuvenation of spirit.

Thoughts * Impressions * Musings * Flow

Letting Go: Loss, Surrender, Mourning and Release.

What does "surrender" mean to you?

let's go deeper. Where did this belief originally come from?

So, what is true surrender?

What are the implications of truly surrendering?

Do you feel...

fear

defeat

joy

release

peace...

Thoughts * Impressions * Musings * Flow

Who will you become once you surrender?

"I'm not giving up, I'm just giving in..."

What will change once you finally give in?

This is your invitation, your call to surrender, to drop your shoulders, release the weight you've carried all these years and float.

Float. Allow. Flow.

Thoughts * Impressions * Musings * Flow

Close your eyes and inhale. Go back in time to when you were 12. Describe her, what does she look like? Who is this 12 year old?

Details are important, write them below.

Thoughts * Impressions * Musings * Flow

Let's go deeper. Think back to your 5th birthday.
Describe it.
What do you remember most?

How was that experience mirroring the entire experience of your childhood?

Thoughts * Impressions * Musings * Flow

Thoughts * Impressions * Musings * Flow

Who did you hope to become all those years ago?

What dreams do you still hold on to...and which have you had to release?

Thoughts * Impressions * Musings * Flow

Have you mourned the death of these childhood dreams yet? Is it time to do so now?

Breathe in, close your eyes, exhale, release.

Thoughts * Impressions * Musings * Flow

When you were just becoming an adult...you may have been 16 or 18 or 21...

Think back to that time.

Go there now.

And, once your there, write out your

hopes

doubts

dreams

ideals

on the next page, from that fresh perspective...

Thoughts * Impressions * Musings * Flow

Today, how are you different? How are you the same? What has surprised you the most?

...today, my
hopes
doubts
ideals
dreams
ARE...

Write them out in RED ink on the following pages.

Thoughts * Impressions * Musings * Flow

Thoughts * Impressions * Musings * Flow

Thoughts * Impressions * Musings * Flow

What are the parts of you that you were forced to leave behind, reject, let go of, close the door on?

yes.

Where did they go, those hidden parts of you?

Close your eyes and search for each one.

Thoughts * Impressions * Musings * Flow

Do you miss these parts of you?

Speak to them now.
Talk to each one, out loud if you can.
Name them, acknowledge them,

honor

each

one

individually.

Thoughts * Impressions * Musings * Flow

Has the time come for them to return, those long forgotten, rejected parts of you?

Yes.

Invite them in.

Welcome them.

Describe them in their newfound place of acceptance and love on the following page...

Thoughts * Impressions * Musings * Flow

How do you feel about the YOU
that YOU used to be?

Who is she/he?

Where is she/he.

Thoughts * Impressions * Musings * Flow

Do you remember those unfulfilled desires?
Those you gave up on long ago...
What were they?

Go back and circle the desires that you still hold dear, the ones that you refuse to throw away. Those ones, they are your true north.

listen and hear and know...

Thoughts * Impressions * Musings * Flow

Thoughts * Impressions * Musings * Flow

There is something you must now release.
What is it time to let go of?

(this can be a comprehensive list)

And now, the time has come...
WHAT HAS BEEN REAWAKENED WITHIN YOU!??

How are you different right now, in this moment?

How are you the same?

How does all of this make you feel?

Thoughts * Impressions * Musings * Flow

You've had to let go, you've had to release, there were things that you've found and those that you have now buried.

It is time to mourn, to actively mourn that which you are consciously releasing. It is akin to death, this process, and mourning is essential.

And so, we mourn.

Create a ritual you will use today to mourn all of the things you haven't allowed yourself the space to grieve for.

Describe your ritual below and keep these instructions for further reference.

Thoughts * Impressions * Musings * Flow

Thoughts * Impressions * Musings * Flow

Who do you need to forgive?

Are you ready to do so, right now?

Fill in the blanks (with red ink if you're up for empowering it with that goddess flow!)

I now forgive _____ for

I forgive you and I set you free. We are both released.

I now forgive _____ for

I forgive you and I set you free. We are both released.

I now forgive _____ for

I forgive you and I set you free. We are both released.

I now forgive   for

I forgive you and I set you free. We are both released.

I now forgive   for

I forgive you and I set you free. We are both released.

I now forgive   for

I forgive you and I set you free. We are both released.

I now forgive   for

I forgive you and I set you free. We are both released.

I now forgive MYSELF for

I forgive you and I set you free. We are both released.

Thoughts * Impressions * Musings * Flow

Self Forgiveness Ritual:

Face a mirror

Look deep into your own eyes.

State, out loud, in a clear and powerful voice.

"I forgive you"
"I am sorry"
"The punishment is over"
"You are inherently good in every single way"
"I love you and I always will"

Allow what every comes to come. Release the emotions once you've acknowledged them.

Release.

Flow.

Breathe.

Thoughts * Impressions * Musings * Flow

Thoughts * Impressions * Musings * Flow

Thoughts * Impressions * Musings * Flow

Think back to what your greatest losses have been in this lifetime.

List them bellow.

Circle the one that still haunts you.

What about the experience of this loss do you still need to release?

Who will you become
once you let go of that pain?

Who are you still holding on to when you know
you should really, really

just

let

Them

go.

How is holding on so tight preventing your flow?

Are there any positive benefits to not letting go?

Is there anything else coming up now?

Thoughts * Impressions * Musings * Flow

Who must you let go of in order to move freely?

Are you willing to?

What must you lose, release, let go of and surrender in order to allow the new to enter in and flourish?

list it, describe it, all of it, in detail...

Thoughts * Impressions * Musings * Flow

Thoughts * Impressions * Musings * Flow

THE RELEASING RITUAL.

GO THROUGH AND UNDERLINE ALL OF THE THINGS, THOUGHTS, PEOPLE, PLACES, EXPERIENCES, EVENTS AND EMOTIONS IN THE PREVIOUS PAGES THAT YOU ARE GOING TO RELEASE AND LET GO OF FULLY.

WRITE A LETTER TO THE UNIVERSAL WHOLE STATING YOUR INTENTION TO LET GO AND LIST EACH ITEM THAT YOU ARE RELEASING. SING THE LETTER.

SPRINKLE THE LETTER WITH A HEAPING OF SEA SALT AND DRIED MINT LEAVES.

BURN THE MIXTURE AND THE LETTER.

BLOW AWAY THE ASHES AND LET THE WINDS TAKE THEM TO THE EARTH.

(SEE NEXT PAGE)

SPRINKLE YOUR HEAD AND BODY WITH SEA SALT AND TAKE A LONG, CLEANSING SHOWER.

THE PROCESS IS NOW COMPLETE. YOU ARE CLEANSED, RENEWED AND READY TO MOVE FORWARD, ACCEPT AND CREATE AND LIVE FULLY

How do you feel, in this moment, right now!?

describe using words...

draw it out in full color

express it via a sound...

Thoughts * Impressions * Musings * Flow

Close your eyes and breathe in life. Place your right hand on your solar plexus and scan your body. How does it feel?

Breathe out and release.

Continue breathing and releasing.

Thoughts * Impressions * Musings * Flow

Emptiness.

Is it bad...good...simply IS.

What is it? What does it look like for YOU?

Take time to savor the emptiness. You've released so very much. Languish in the nothingness for now. There is sacred beauty in the space that is created once you release that which has passed on.

Create a ritual, a celebration to commemorate your courage in letting go.

Welcome in the sacred emptiness.

Allow it.

Thoughts * Impressions * Musings * Flow

Thoughts * Impressions * Musings * Flow

Seeing YOU: recovering your True Truth and creating your world anew.

Seeing YOU, the ritual

Take this book into the bathroom with you. Close the door behind you and make sure you are able to have 15-30 minutes of uninterrupted alone time, just you, the mirror and this book.

Set a timer for 10 minutes and do nothing but look into the mirror and observe your reflection. Look deeper. Continue to look at your face, stare into your eyes and do not look away until the timer goes off.

Allow yourself the time and dedication to your own reflection. Allow yourself to connect into your soul via your eyes.

On the following pages, write down everything you see, sense and experience during this exercise.

Thoughts * Impressions * Musings * Flow

Thoughts * Impressions * Musings * Flow

Thoughts * Impressions * Musings * Flow

How do you truly see yourself?
Describe the person you believe you are...

list your flaws.

Go back and reread the last page.
Are those really flaws?
Are you sure?
Why?

Do you accept these things?
Do you see them as blemished or badges of honor?

Are you beautiful?

Count all of the facets of your beauty...

the facets of your beauty...

What is true beauty?

What are your favorite things about your

face

and

body...

Thoughts * Impressions * Musings * Flow

Thoughts * Impressions * Musings * Flow

What are all of the truly beautiful things that blossom from your soul.

Your soul is breathtakingly beautiful, recount the ways in takes your breath away below.

Thoughts * Impressions * Musings * Flow

Describe the beauty that is present in your life right now.

Describe the beauty and magnificence you're ready and willing to create in your life now and from this moment forward.

Thoughts * Impressions * Musings * Flow

Thoughts * Impressions * Musings * Flow

What is the beauty that you carry hidden really deep inside you? I mean the type of beauty rarely witnessed, rarely seen.

Describe it.

Thoughts * Impressions * Musings * Flow

What have you been hiding?

What else?

Anything else...look deep, deeper still.

Thoughts * Impressions * Musings * Flow

Thoughts * Impressions * Musings * Flow

We've uncovered this for a reason.
The time has come for you to release
your
brilliance.

Are you ready to come out of hiding yet?

Thoughts * Impressions * Musings * Flow

What will happen once the whole of you is finally released?

Thoughts * Impressions * Musings * Flow

The force that is within you, what is it?
What does it feel like?
What is it called?

What happens once this force within you is fully unleashed on to the world?

Breathe in.

Exhale.

Breathe in deeper.

Exhale slowly.

Again.

Thoughts * Impressions * Musings * Flow

Get ready.

Thoughts *Impressions *Musings *Flow

The time has come to unleash your greatness upon this world.
We've been waiting for you.
It's time.

Thoughts * Impressions * Musings * Flow

Describe, in detail, what the NEW YOU looks like, feels like, moves like.

A Newer You...

A Newer You...

A Newer You...

Describe, in detail, what a typical day in your ideal life is...

Ideal Day AM...

Ideal Day Midday...

Ideal Day PM...

DELFINA ALDEN

My Ideal Night...

Thoughts * Impressions * Musings * Flow

Thoughts * Impressions * Musings * Flow

Thoughts * Impressions * Musings * Flow

THE CLOSING RITUAL. (THIS ONE'S A MUST)

HO'OPONOPONO, AS YOU MAY KNOW IS AN ANCIENT FORGIVENESS RITUAL PRACTICED AND PERFORMED ON ISLANDS THROUGHOUT THE SOUTH PACIFIC, INCLUDING SAMOA, TAHITI AND NEW ZEALAND. IT IS PROFOUND AND IT IS PURE MAGIC. HERE, WE WILL MULTIPLY THE HO'OPONOPONO PRACTICE BY INCORPORATING SOME SELF LOVE AND DIVINE LEVEL CREATIVE CARE ALONG WITH THE ANCIENT RITUAL PRACTICE. DOING THIS WILL ABSOLUTELY CHANGE YOUR LIFE. AND, YOU ARE READY FOR IT, I PROMISE.

SET ASIDE AN HOUR OF SELF TIME. MAKE SURE THAT YOU WILL BE ALONE AND UNDISTURBED FOR THIS ENTIRE TIME. POSITION A FULL LENGTH MIRROR IN FRONT OF THE SPACE YOU ARE PREPARING FOR YOURSELF. LAY DOWN BLANKETS AND TOWELS. LIGHT CANDLES AND INCENSE AND CREATE A SPACE OF COMFORT, WARMTH AND BEAUTY. YOU MAY BRING FRESH FLOWERS INTO THE SPACE. CRYSTALS, PICTURES, DEITIES

AND TALISMANS MAY ALSO PRESIDE OVER THIS RITUAL. KEEP WHAT FEELS RIGHT, REMOVE ANYTHING THAT FEELS UNNECESSARY. YOU ARE CREATING A SACRED SPACE FOR YOURSELF. WHAT YOU ARE ABOUT TO DO, WHILE SEEMINGLY SIMPLE. IS AN EXERCISE THAT HAS INCREDIBLE RAMIFICATIONS AND IS POSSIBLY A ONCE IN A LIFETIME EXPERIENCE.

PREPARE YOUR ANOINTING OIL. YOU MAY USE COCONUT OIL AS A BASE AND MIX IN ROSE OIL IN ORDER TO INFUSE IT WITH LOVE VIBRATIONS. AS YOU MIX THE OIL, CLOSE YOUR EYES AND SAY A PRAYER OF LOVE AND DEVOTION TO THE GODDESS OF LOVE, PLEASURE, HEALTH AND WELL BEING. DECLARE THAT THE CONCOCTION YOU HOLD IN YOUR HANDS IS A MIRACLE HEALING BALM.

AND, SO IT IS.

REMOVE ALL OF YOUR CLOTHING. YUP, GET COMPLETELY NAKED. WATCH YOURSELF UNDRESS IN THE FULL LENGTH MIRROR. STARE AT YOUR REFLECTION. LOOK INTO YOUR EYES

ONCE MORE, PLACE HANDS IN PRAYER POSE AND PLACE THEM AT YOUR HEART CENTER. BOW TO YOUR REFLECTIONS IN HONOR OF YOU, YOUR ENTIRE BEING, YOUR HIGHEST SELF AND THE MAGNIFICENCE THAT YOU TRULY ARE.

NOW, PLACE THE ANOINTED OIL MIXTURE IN THE PALM OF YOUR HAND AND BEGIN TO MASSAGE YOUR FOOT, STARTING AT THE TIPS OF YOUR TOES AND PROGRESSING TOWARDS YOUR HEELS AND ANKLES. MASSAGE GENTLY, MASSAGE WITH PURPOSE AND LOVE. AND, REPEAT THE FOLLOWING WORDS, DIRECTING THEM AT EACH PART OF YOUR BEAUTIFUL, SACRED BODY:
"I'M SORRY, PLEASE FORGIVE ME, I LOVE YOU, THANK YOU"

DO THIS MASSAGE AND SACRED OFFERING TO EACH PART OF YOUR BODY UNTIL YOU REACH THE TOP OF YOUR HEAD. BE SURE TO PAY SPECIAL ATTENTION TO YOUR GENITALS.

BE GENTLE WITH YOURSELF DURING THIS PRACTICE AND ALLOW ANY AND ALL EMOTIONS TO FLOW FREELY. BE TRUE TO THE EXPRESSION OF YOUR EMOTIONS. ALLOW THE LAUGHTER, ALLOW THE TEARS, THE PRIMAL SCREAMS, SHRIEKS AND GROANS.
ALLOW IT ALL.

ONCE YOU HAVE MASSAGED, EVERY SQUARE INCH OF YOUR BEAUTIFUL BODY AND HAVE SAID THE SACRED PRAYER AND COMPLETED THE RITUAL. TURN TO THE MIRROR ONCE AGAIN. THIS TIME VIEW YOURSELF WITH THE LOVE, COMPASSION AND KNOWING OF YOUR HIGHEST SELF. STARE INTO YOUR EYES AND WELCOME YOU INTO YOUR ARMS. ALLOW THIS SACRED REUNION. WELCOME YOU INTO THIS NEW PLACE OF TRUE, FULL UNCONDITIONAL LOVE.

YOU ARE HERE.

YOU ARE LOVED.

YOU ARE HOME.

Thoughts * Impressions * Musings * Flow

Thoughts * Impressions * Musings * Flow

Made in the USA
Middletown, DE
26 December 2016